Gabriel's Christmas Journey

The First Advent

Gabriel's Christmas Journey

The First Advent

Written by
Dianne Spotts

Illustrated by
John Conning

Copyright © 2017 by Dianne Spotts

All rights reserved. No part of this book may be reproduced or utilized in any form or by any means, electronic or mechanical, including photocopying, recording or by any information or storage retrieval system, without permission in writing from the publisher.

ISBN-13: 978-1979848541

ISBN-10: 1979848548

WCP
Pearl S. Buck Writing Center Press
520 Dublin Road, Perkasie, Pennsylvania 18944
www.psbwritingcenter.org

Dedication

I dedicate this book with love and appreciation to the angels and cherubs in my immediate and extended family.

A cherub dashed into the choir loft and tugged on the angel Gabriel's wing while he was directing the heavenly choir.

"Gabriel," the cherub said, "God wants to see you, *right now.*"
"Oh, no! What did I do?" Gabriel trembled and, in a New Jerusalem minute, he was in the brilliant light of God's throne room.

Hello, Gabriel." God said, "Catch your breath, and sit down for a moment. I want to tell you about a special mission on earth to…"

"Earth? MMMe? It's been a a a long time," stammered Gabriel.

"Yes," God replied, "since you visited Daniel and . . ."

"Daniel? Oh, my dearest Lord, does this have anything to do with lions?"

"No, Gabe. You'll visit some wonderful people and announce…"

"Talk? NNNot sing? Oh, Oh, forgive me, but my good Lord, you know how…

"Gabe, if you keep interrupting me you're going to end up in bad weather patterns all the way to earth!"

"SSSorry, my Lord."

"Set your music aside for now. You're going on the road to bring great news to some special people."

"But, but, what will I say? You know I get nervous when I …"

"Gabe, for eternity's sake, you've been here for more than half of forever and still you worry! Now listen, trust me, won't you, please?"

"Yes, Lord, I will."

"Would you like Cherub to keep you company?"
"Oh yes, Lord. Thank you."

"Your first stop will be at my Temple in Jerusalem to see my priest, Zechariah, to announce that he and his wife Elizabeth, who are old and have no children, will have a son."

"Wow! I guess he'll be pretty excited!"

"Actually, he won't believe you. And you'll find *he* interrupts too. Oh, and before you leave him, remind him of the story of Abraham and Sarah."

"Oh, I remember them. I guess I can handle *that*."

Gabriel arrives at the Temple and greets Zechariah:

"HHHello, Zechariah. I am Gabriel and have been sent to give you good news. God has heard your prayer. Your wife Elizabeth will have a son."

"How can this be? I am an old man."

"BBBecause you do not believe me, you will not be able to speak until after your son is born - and you are to call him John.

Remember Abraham & Sarah? They too were very old when Isaac was born."

Meanwhile, back in the throne room, God congratulates Gabriel.

"Good, Gabe! You were a little nervous, but you did fine. Next, I want you to visit Mary, a precious girl, who is to be the Mother of My Son."

"My word!" Gabe answered.

"More accurately, Gabe, He is *My Word*, and He will live among *My* people."

"Far Out, Sir! I mean, that's exciting! *Your very own Son – Your Word!* I'll bet that's the most important message of the eons! You must love Mary a great deal to give her this privilege. Will *she* believe me?"

"Yes, she will. Then tell her about her cousin, Elizabeth."

"Great. That will help her believe *her* miracle."

"Exactly, Gabe."

Back in the Throne Room, God congratulates Gabriel. "Gabe, you're doing very well.

"Next, you will visit Joseph, Mary's husband, in a dream. He will help her raise My Son."

"Well, Gabe, your mission is almost complete. Your last stop will be the fields outside of Bethlehem where shepherds are guarding the sheep and lambs that are to be sacrificed in My temple. Tell them that *The* Lamb of God, Mary's baby boy, has been born. They'll want to go see Him for themselves."

"May I go to see Him too, Lord?"

Gabriel appears to the shepherds on the hills overlooking Bethlehem.

"Do not be afraid, I bring you good news of great joy.

Your *Savior* has been born!"

"Thank you, Cherub, I couldn't have done this without you.

Now it's time to sing!
Glory to God in the Highest!

Bible Sources from the NRSV
(New Revised Standard Version)

Daniel	Daniel 14:31-42
Zechariah	Luke 1:7-20, 59-66
Abraham & Sarah	Genesis 15:4-6, 21:1-7 and 18:9-15
Mary	Luke 1:26-38
Elizabeth	Luke 1:24, 39-45, 57
Joseph	Matthew 1:18-25
Shepherds & Fields	Luke 2:8-20
Nativity	Luke 2:6-13

Lessons Learned

Were you ever asked to do
something that made you nervous?

Did you ask a friend or your parent
to help you?

Have you ever helped someone
who was worried?

Do you remember to pray
if you are scared?

Remember, you can call on
your guardian angel for help too.

Acknowledgements

Without the expertise and generous assistance of Dr. Anne Kaler, Senior Editor of WCP, and Linda Donaldson, Layout and Design Editor of WCP, Gabriel could not have taken flight. John Conning added the magic that made this into the book you have in your hands.

After her retirement, **Dianne Spotts**, a widow, mother, grandmother and great grandmother began freelancing articles to both secular and Christian magazines, newspapers and anthologies. She has facilitated Memoir Writing workshops, led prayer meetings, written for her parish quarterly newsletter, and is a church musician. Follow her future publishing projects at www.LambByLamb.com.

John Conning is an animator and illustrator who works on video and TV shows for MTV, History Channel, Cartoon Network, HBO, Marvel and Sony TV. He is currently developing a new project featuring his talented cats. Learn more about John's work at www.memethecat.com.

Made in the USA
Middletown, DE
09 December 2018